WORLD*focus*

Senegal

ALISON BROWNLIE

Contents

Introduction

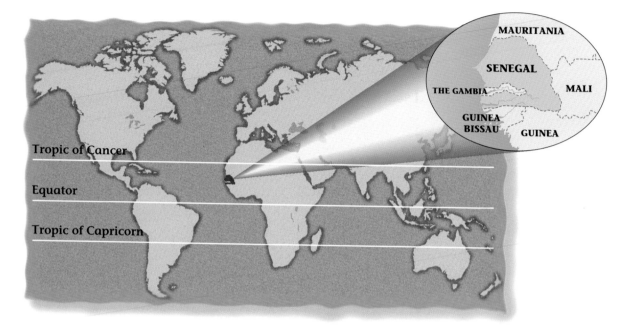

You may not have heard very much about Senegal. It's not often mentioned on the news. That doesn't mean that nothing happens there or that it isn't an interesting country. In this book you will learn something about this country, its rich culture, and its people.

△ **Where is Senegal?**

About the country

Senegal is the most westerly country on the continent of Africa. If you stand on the shore and look out across the Atlantic Ocean, there is nothing between you and the Americas. From here you can see beautiful sunsets over the sea. People have called Senegal 'the Land of the Setting Sun'.

Look at the map above. You can see that another country, the Gambia, lies within Senegal. It follows the River Gambia and slots into Senegal like a sleeve. It is almost an **enclave**. The south-west of Senegal is therefore separated from the rest of the country.

Senegal is one of the smaller countries in Africa. It is just a little bigger than England and Wales put together, but with a much smaller population of 8 million. It is a very flat country.

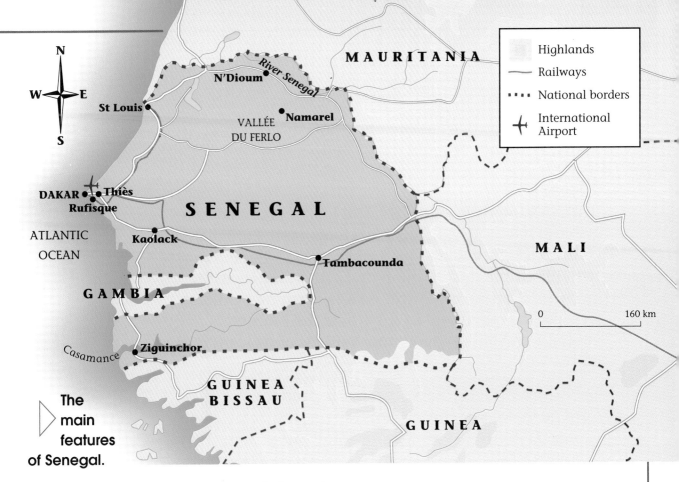

Highlands
Railways
National borders
International Airport

MAURITANIA

River Senegal

N'Dioum

St Louis

VALLÉE DU FERLO

Namarel

SENEGAL

DAKAR
Thiès
Rufisque

ATLANTIC OCEAN

Kaolack

Tambacounda

MALI

GAMBIA

0   160 km

Casamance
Ziguinchor

GUINEA BISSAU

GUINEA

▷ The main features of Senegal.

▽ One of Senegal's beautiful beaches on the Atlantic coast.

Forests and deserts

Senegal has a **tropical** climate but it varies quite a lot. In the south-west it is hot and wet. It is on the edge of the **monsoon** area and has four to five months of rain, almost three times as much rain as Dakar, on the coast.

There are dense forests, and **mangrove** creeks and also a fantastic variety of birdlife, including flamingos, pelicans and herons. Many birds that we see in Britain during the summer spend their winters in Senegal.

The north is also hot but it is part of the **Sahel**, on the edge of the Sahara desert, and it is very dry. Rain falls only between July and October. And even then people don't know exactly when, or if, it will rain. The soil is sandy and the hot **harmattan** winds cause sandstorms which go on for days.

3

The people

People have lived in the area now called Senegal for many thousands of years.

Recent history

In 1450 Europeans visited Senegal looking for gold and precious metals. Then, 100 years later, more Europeans came to take people to the Caribbean to work on plantations producing cotton and sugar for people in Europe. All over West Africa, men, women and children were captured and sent in ships over the Atlantic Ocean in appalling conditions. Millions of Africans died on the way.

Today, many black people in the USA and the Caribbean are descended from these slaves. Some come to Senegal to see where their ancestors came from. They usually visit the Isle of Gorée.

Senegal was a colony of France from the middle of the nineteenth century until 1960, when it became independent. The French considered it as part of France and people born in certain towns were full French citizens.

▽ Slave house on Gorée, which was a collecting station for slaves.

People and language

The people of Senegal belong to many different groups – the Wolof, Peulh, Serer, Toucouleur, Mandinga and Diola. Two million people belong to the largest ethnic group, the Wolof. There are six national languages but 80 per cent of the people speak Wolof. Children in schools are taught in French, which is the official language, but it is unusual to hear people speaking it outside the main towns.

Politics and religion

Most people in Senegal are **Muslims**. The Muslim leaders, called marabouts, are a very powerful group in Senegal.

△ Senegal's daily newspaper is called 'Le Soleil', which is French for 'The Sun'.

Senegal is a **multi-party democracy** and has a good **human rights** reputation, although the government has not always lived up to this. Newspapers in Senegal are allowed to say what they want and there are active trade unions. These are all signs that the government believes its people should have freedom of expression.

Culture

In Senegal there is a rich **oral tradition** where stories and histories are told by **griots**. People say that when a griot dies it is like a library burning down because of all the stories that are lost. The stringed kora and talking drum are popular instruments and music is played at every opportunity. Senegal has several world-famous musicians including Youssou N'dour and Baba Maal.

Where do people live?

▷ Dakar, with the Isle of Gorée in the background.

In Senegal more people live in towns than they do in most other African countries. Almost half the population live in Dakar, the capital, and towns like Thiès, Ziguinchor, Kaolack and St. Louis.

Living in the country

Most people living in country villages grow food or keep animals. In areas where there is more rain and the land is fertile, there are more villages. In the north, where it rains less, the people are **nomadic** for part of the year. Most villages have a school and a health centre but a few do not. Some children cannot go to school because the schools are too far away.

Sometimes after a bad **drought** crops may die so there is little food to eat. People leave their villages to look for work in the cities or towns, or even abroad. It is often men who go, sending money back to the women who look after the family. If they can, people living in the city go back to their village to help with cattle or the crops at busy times.

Living in the city

Dakar, the capital city, is built on a **peninsula** and is cooled by sea breezes. It has high-rise office blocks, hotels, restaurants, elegant shops and traffic jams. Some people think Dakar is a lot like Paris. You can even buy French baguettes for breakfast! It is also an important sea port, **exporting** groundnuts (peanuts) and fish products, and importing manufactured goods that the country needs.

△ A delivery of baguettes to a village.

Dakar is growing very quickly as people leave the countryside and come to the city. Many of them live in areas of poor housing on the outskirts of the city, known as 'bidonvilles' or shanty towns. There are few jobs and many people are already unemployed. People find whatever work they can. Many women have set up small businesses such as hair plaiting, doughnut making and selling fruit in the market. There are many beggars asking for money. In Muslim culture giving to the poor is very important and people give money readily.

▽ Shops in Dakar.

Agriculture

Many people, both women and men, are farmers of one kind or another. They may grow their own food, keep animals or work on large farms and plantations where groundnuts (peanuts) and cotton are grown.

Food for the family

In Senegal men own the land but women do almost all the work and produce the food the family needs. In the south people work on small plots of land and grow maize, **sorghum**, millet and rice. In the north, where the dry climate makes it difficult to grow many crops, people keep animals for their milk. On special occasions a goat may be killed, otherwise meat is rarely eaten. On the coast many people make a living from fishing.

Groundnuts

The main crops which Senegal produces to sell abroad are cotton, rice and groundnuts. However, the growing of groundnuts has meant that trees have had to be cut down on a large scale in order to clear the land.

▽ When a cow is milked, only a little is taken, leaving plenty for the calf.

△ Groundnut mountain. Groundnuts are exported and used to make groundnut oil.

Growing groundnuts year after year is not good for the soil and they use up land that could be used for growing food crops. This means that Senegal has to buy more food from other countries.

The price of food

Senegal grows two-thirds of the food it needs and buys the rest from other countries, such as rice from South-east Asia. Until recently, economic policies have meant that imported food was quite cheap making it difficult for local farmers to compete. In 1994, however, Senegalese money became less valuable than money in other countries. This meant that things bought from abroad were more expensive. As a result people are now buying more local goods.

Drought and locusts

In many places the climate makes it difficult to grow crops. It doesn't rain as much as it did 20 years ago. Regular **droughts** create enormous problems, but are not the only problem that farmers face. Sometimes crops are ruined by plagues of locusts, which can eat a farmer's entire crop overnight.

Industry

Industry in Senegal is changing. The closing down of many factories has meant that many people have lost their jobs. New industries, such as tourism and film-making, have not yet created enough new jobs.

Mineral resources

As Senegal has no resources which can be used to make energy, it must import oil. In the ground in east Senegal there is iron ore, copper, gold and marble which could bring in a lot of money for the country. Unfortunately they are in very remote areas and it would cost a great deal to mine and use the minerals at present. Phosphates, which are used to make fertilizers, are mined near Thiès and are a major export.

△ Working on a loom to make fabric.

Industry today

When Senegal was a colony of France many factories were set up to produce goods to sell to other countries in West Africa. These countries have now set up their own industries and no longer need to buy things from Senegal. Many factories have closed down in Senegal and things which used to be made here no longer are, for example shoes and galvanized sheet metal.

In the past some of Senegal's industries were set up to process imported goods, like refineries for processing oil. These are now very old, out-dated and run-down and the government cannot afford to repair them.

Making a living

With so much unemployment people do whatever they can to earn a little money. In the markets of Dakar you will find people weaving baskets, chiselling out wooden bowls or even hammering together briefcases made from old beer cans. Oxfam supports women's groups who set up small businesses doing things like dyeing material, raising chickens and making leather belts.

Tourism

Senegal has a well-developed tourist industry with 200,000 visitors a year, mainly from France and Germany. The country's attractions include its beautiful sandy beaches, the excellent climate, and animal and bird reserves. Unfortunately, much of the tourist industry's profits goes to the foreign companies who own the leisure centres in Senegal.

▽ Senegal's birdlife provides much interest for tourists.

Challenges

All over the world countries face problems and difficulties. Senegal is no exception.

Drought

Since 1970 the **Sahel** has suffered an almost continuous **drought**. Many wells and rivers have dried up and people find it more and more difficult to grow food for themselves. Some people think that these are the effects of **global warming** and that the drop in rainfall is due to car fumes and industries in Europe.

Foreign debt

Like many other countries, one of the biggest problems facing Senegal is the amount of money borrowed from other countries to develop. In order to repay the debt the government has had to stop spending on many things.

No new schools have been built which means that many children cannot go to school and those who can are in very large classes with few books. The government can no longer afford to pay important people such as doctors, teachers and agricultural advisors.

The problem of the foreign debt has affected people in different ways. The fisherfolk of St Louis are finding that their catch is much smaller than it was a few years ago.

They have little for themselves to eat and even less to sell on the market. This is because large, modern European ships are catching most of the fish. It used to be illegal for European boats to fish off the coast of Senegal, but because the government needs money it agreed that the Europeans could pay for the right to fish here. The fisherfolk of St Louis get none of this money.

Overcoming poverty

Most people are determined to improve their lives. In towns and villages they have joined together to form self-help groups. Some groups have set up a club where everyone puts a little money in every month. They take it in turns to borrow some of the money, for example, for an emergency or to help start a small business. Other groups seek advice and information from experts about looking after their animals.

◁ People in Senegal know that being able to read and write will give them confidence and independence.

▽ The fishing boats are called pirogues. They are sometimes used for racing.

Namarel

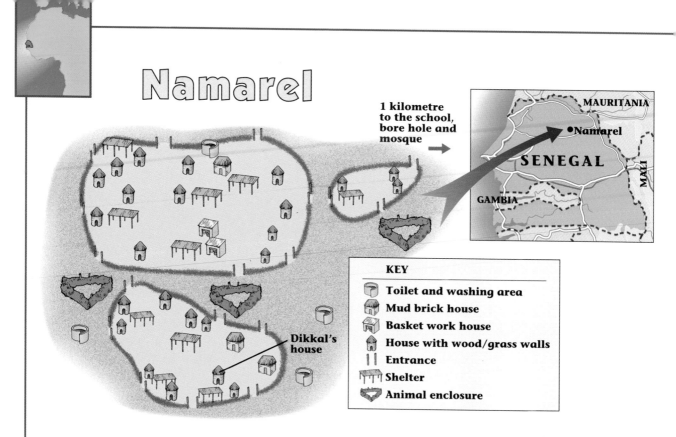

1 kilometre to the school, bore hole and mosque →

KEY
- 🛢 Toilet and washing area
- 🏠 Mud brick house
- 🏠 Basket work house
- 🏠 House with wood/grass walls
- ‖ Entrance
- ⛺ Shelter
- ⬨ Animal enclosure

Dikkal's house

MAURITANIA
•Namarel
SENEGAL
MALI
GAMBIA

△ Map of Namarel showing where Dikkal Sow lives.

The village of Namarel lies in the Ferlo region of northern Senegal.

To get to Namarel from the nearest town 60 kilometres away, you travel on a road which is no more than a track, across a flat landscape of sandy soil and low-lying shrubs. Every now and then you see a baobab tree, often called 'an upside-down tree' because it looks as though it has its roots in the air. In a landscape like this, where everything looks the same, it would be very difficult for you to find the village but Mustapha Dia, who comes from this area says 'When you've lived here all your life you can navigate by the sun, and by using signs – trees, the way the land looks.'

The climate in Namarel

The Ferlo is part of the **Sahel**. The wet season is between July and October but rain is unreliable and quickly soaked up by the dry sandy soil. The **harmattan** wind blows from the Sahara desert causing sandstorms so fierce, you cannot see your hand in front of your face. Between March and July, the hotseason, daytime temperatures can be as high as 45° C.

▷ Animals are brought to the well at Namarel for watering.

Many people living in Namarel can remember a time when the rainfall was much higher and many different types of plants grew. In the last 20 years though, the climate has changed and there is now much less rain.

Dikkal with her elder brother and his baby.

Dikkal Sow

Dikkal Sow loves living in Namarel. She loves the landscape and she loves her family and her many friends. People in Namarel always look after each other.

Dikkal Sow is eight. She is the youngest in her family. She has two brothers and two sisters. Her parents own some **irrigated** millet fields near the Senegal River, 60 kilometres away, and they are often away looking after the crops. Dikkal has plenty of aunts and uncles to look after her.

Village life

The people

The people who live in Namarel are the Peulh people. They are **semi-nomadic pastoralists**. During the dry season some of them move around the region with their animals, mainly cows and goats, in search of water and food. Sometimes their wicker huts can be seen near the Senegal River during the dry season. During the wet season they return to their villages. The money the herders get from selling their animals is their main income.

△ Water is collected from deep wells.

Many young people leave Namarel to look for work in Dakar, or even as far away as Paris in France. But people always keep in touch with their village and, if they can, they return to help their village. A group of people from Namarel who were studying in Dakar set up an organization called ADENA which runs many activities like health, agriculture and literacy training in the area. Oxfam supports ADENA.

△ Ousseynou Wally, the local carpenter making a bed from branches lashed together.

The place

Dikkal's village is made up of three large compounds where members of her **extended family** live. The houses are made out of natural materials – mud bricks, wood and woven grass. These houses are cooler than the concrete buildings in the village, like the school, the dispensary (where medicines are given out) and the millet store.

There are four small shops in Namarel which sell rice and dried fish. But these things are expensive as they have to be brought from far away. If people want anything else, such as clothing, they have to travel a long way to one of the towns. Apart from this people are more or less **self-sufficient**.

People in Namarel cannot take water for granted like we do. They don't get it from a tap but from pumps in deep bore holes which have to be drilled. People in Namarel pay for the water they use and this money is used to keep the pump in a good state of repair.

School

The school in Namarel is one of the few concrete buildings in the village. Dikkal has been going to school for four months but she says she hasn't really got used to it yet! Because the government can only afford one teacher for the school, only a third of the children can go at any one time. And only children who live in Namarel or near enough to walk can go as there is no transport. In the classroom there are very few books and pens.

School subjects

There are 44 pupils in Dikkal's class. Most of the class are the same age as her but there are also some 14-year-olds who are learning different things from the others. They are studying for their Elementary School Certificate and entrance exam for secondary school. They study French, mathematics, the history and geography of Senegal and Africa, and drawing and singing. To take the exam pupils must go to N'Dioum, 60 kilometres away, but some may be unable to pay for the transport to get them there.

▽ Dikkal's classroom.

 Dikkal's group learn reading, writing, mathematics, singing and sport.

Alassane Diouf, the teacher, teaches the children things which will be useful to them in their home lives, such as how to grow vegetables and build stoves that don't burn too much wood, and how to help their parents at home. He sometimes buys pens and books out of his own salary for the children to use.

Language

Although Dikkal speaks Pulaar at home with her family, at school she is taught in French. As she doesn't understand French the teacher has to help her a lot. Many adults are now going to classes to learn to read and write in their own language of Pulaar as they were never taught how to when they went to school. Being able to read and write is very important as it means people don't have to ask others to read things for them. It gives them more independence. It is only recently that books began to be produced in the Pulaar language and they are very popular.

Spare time

Dikkal does lots of jobs to help her family and sometimes there isn't a lot of time left for playing games. Luckily, Dikkal enjoys many of her chores.

Playing games

When she does have some spare time, Dikkal likes playing a game called tenge. She throws a stone in the air and has to pick up other stones in ones or twos before it lands. It's very similar to a game called fivestones or jacks. Dikkal has lots of friends and they like playing with dolls together. They pretend the dolls are real children and they make the dolls fetch water and wood just like they do. But Dikkal doesn't make her doll go to school!

△ Dikkal playing tenge in the doorway of her home.

Festivals

Ramadan is a very special month of the year when Muslims **fast**. Dikkal is too young to fast but she will when she is 15. People who are fasting go without food and drink from sunrise until sunset.

Juulde Korka is a festival which takes place at the end of Ramadan. It is known as Eid-ul-Fitr by Muslims in other countries. Each family celebrates by eating, singing, and dancing. Dikkal enjoys the celebrations very much because she says 'everyone is happy'.

The cultural group

There are no phones in Namarel, not even a local radio station, although they are hoping to start one soon. However, it is not difficult to find out about local news.

A group of musicians travel from village to village singing songs about the past, the Peulh culture and things that have happened in other villages, such as a baby being born. They also sing songs about environmental issues to help people to care for the land. Their show includes singing and drumming and they are very popular. Mbourel Dia, the main singer, is a **griotte**.

▽ Dikkal enjoys learning songs about the Peulh people and their history from the cultural group.

When there are visitors in the village they are always offered food, drink and somewhere to stay. People eat together from a large dish. The villagers make sure the guest gets the best bits of food. After the meal the traditional three cups of strong sweet mint tea are brewed and then poured into small cups from a height so that it is frothy.

A day with Dikkal

Getting up and going to school

Dikkal is woken up by her aunt before sunrise. This is the coolest part of the day and people get up early to get their jobs done before it is too hot. Outside the compound is a fenced-off area where Dikkal washes using a cup to pour water from a bucket over herself.

Dikkal walks to school with her friends and gets there by 8 a.m. At mid-morning pupils have their breakfast. The reason it is so late is that they have to wait for the cattle to be brought in and milked.

Afternoon chores

School finishes at 1 p.m. and Dikkal goes home to eat lunch and do her chores. She prefers working at home than going to school. Dikkal goes out with her friends to fetch wood from a tree called kelli, which burns slowly.

▽ Fary Diallo working at the market garden.

Dikkal helps feed the calves and collects water from the tap just a kilometre away. Water is piped to the tap from the well in Namarel. Dikkal's family is lucky to be near a water source – some people have to walk a long way every day to get water. Sometimes she helps one of her older sisters tend their mother's vegetable patch, where they grow onions and cabbages. Two afternoons a week she has to go back to school for another two hours.

When boys are not at school their job is to look after the animals. Even boys as young as six are responsible for a small herd. They leave with the herd early in the morning and spend the day with the animals looking for food.

Evening relaxation

The evening meal, which Dikkal helps her aunt cook, is usually lacciri. This is a kind of **couscous** made from millet served with milk. Sometimes they have lamb, goat or chicken with the couscous. It is dark by 7 p.m. and there is no electricity. The family sit by the fire talking about the day, telling stories, or they go to visit friends and old people. Caring about old people is very important in Senegal.

△ Dikkal helps her aunt pound the millet for the evening meal.

Travelling around Namarel

In Namarel no one has a car and people get around by walking. Most things that need to be transported round the village are carried. However, people have come up with clever ideas to transport heavier things.

Transporting water

To collect water people fill inner tubes from tractor tyres at the well. These are loaded onto the backs of donkeys or carts. The water is needed for cooking, washing and drinking and also for the animals. In this hot climate everyone needs a lot of water.

Travelling out of the village

Roads into Namarel are nothing more than rough tracks in the sand. Vehicles don't often come along but when a truck does visit the village it is packed with people, taking advantage of the opportunity to visit. If you see another vehicle driving in this area you always stop to chat and find out what the latest news is.

If people need to go the hospital, or to buy or sell things, they have to go to N'Dioum, 60 kilometres away. They usually have to walk and this takes over a day. If they're lucky they might get a lift in a passing vehicle. People cannot use bicycles because the wheels would get stuck in the sand.

A cart hurrying off with its load of water.

Filling inner tubes with water at the borehole.

The costs of transport

Transport is a big problem for people in Namarel. Transport costs push up the price of anything that comes from the towns, making these things very expensive. Everyone in Namarel hopes that ADENA will soon be able to buy a vehicle which people could use to transport animals to the town to sell and to carry goods back. It could also be used as an ambulance.

Journeys around Senegal

If you were to visit Senegal you would probably fly into Yof, the international airport. From here it is a short taxi or bus ride into Dakar, the capital city, just 12 kilometres away.

Getting around Dakar

For those who can afford taxi fares, getting around Dakar is quite easy. For the majority however even bus fares are too expensive and they must walk. There are no pavements or crossings and unfortunately there are many accidents involving pedestrians. More accidents are caused because many buses are old, in a poor state and unsafe.

Buses

Buses travel from Dakar to and between all the major towns. People on the buses will be visiting friends in another town, going to Dakar to look for work, or returning to their village to help out on the land.

▽ You will often see buses on the main roads with luggage piled high on their roofs.

The ferry

Le Joola ferry sails twice a week in each direction between Dakar and Basse Casamance. The journey takes seventeen hours but is a lot easier than travelling overland. The ferry is an important route for traders taking goods to and from Senegal's capital. It sometimes seems more like a floating market than a boat with its cargo of fruit and vegetables, live chickens, dried fish and spices from Casamance and manufactured **consumer goods** from the city.

△ Taxis lined up outside the station in Dakar.

Trains

From the old station right in the centre of Dakar you can get a train to Bamako in Mali, or to the town of St Louis in the north. Thiès is an important train junction and work on the railways provides important employment for the people of the town.

If you could afford it you could go on one of *Air Senegal's* flights to St Louis, Ziguinchor and Tambacounda. Most towns have a small runway but few people can afford to travel by air. They take the bus, the train or the ferry instead.

Images of Senegal

Women work together to support each other and improve their lives.

This man is picking pods to feed his goats.

In a short book like this is it very difficult to tell you everything there is to know about Senegal. It is a country full of many contrasts – of desert and forest, wealth and poverty, city and village.

You will have read of some of the difficulties facing many Senegalese people, especially the poorest. People would be quick to tell you though how they face up to these with strength and determination.

Young men may be forced to leave their village to look for work in the towns.

Many women borrow money from their group to start a small business, such as this market stall.

What you come across everywhere is music and dancing, and people who will always make you welcome and share a joke with you. Even people who own very few things are ready to share what they have. People take great pride in being able to cope with difficult situations and, above all, in sticking together and helping each other.

'Poverty is not being without clothes: the person who is truly poor is the one who has nobody.' Wolof proverb.

Glossary

Colony A country taken over by another one.

Consumer goods Things manufactured in factories that people buy for their homes such as TVs, radios and washing machines.

Couscous A dish of steamed, crushed wheat.

Drought A long period of time with no, or very little rain.

Enclave A country completely surrounded by another.

Exports Goods which are sold to other countries.

Extended family In Western society the nuclear family is more common and includes just parents and children. An extended family is when grandparents, aunts, uncles, cousins and even more distant relations are included in one family unit.

Fast To go without food for a period of time, often for religious reasons.

Global warming The theory that pollution and industrialization are having the effect of increasing the earth's temperatures.

Griottes The people in the community who tell the stories, sometimes by singing.

Harmattan A hot wind which blows from the Sahara desert.

Human rights These are the things that all human beings are entitled to and include the right to be able to say what you want and not to be discriminated against because of your religious or political beliefs.

Irrigation A system of providing water for plants by means of pipes and channels.

Mangrove A group of low trees with exposed roots, usually found in tropical swamps.

Monsoon This is seasonal wind that often brings rain.

Multi-party democracy A political system which means that anyone can set up a political party and ask for people to vote for them.

Muslims Muslims are people who follow the Islamic religion.

Nomadic People who travel around, usually with animals looking for pasture.

Oral tradition The tradition of passing on a community's history from generation to generation by telling stories.

Pastoralists People who make a living from herding animals and selling their products, such as their skins, meat and milk.

Peninsula A piece of land surrounded on three sides by water.

Sahel This is an Arabic word meaning 'on the edge'. It is the area on the edge of the Sahara Desert.

Self-sufficient This is when people are able to grow enough food to feed themselves and their family and produce all the other things that they need without relying on other people.

Semi-nomadic People who travel around for the dry part of the year looking for pasture.

Sorghum A tropical grain.

Tropical A word to describe the part of the world between the tropics of Cancer and Capricorn.

Index

About Oxfam in Senegal

The international family of Oxfams works with poor people and their organizations in over 70 countries. Oxfam believes that all people have basic rights: to earn a living, and to have food, shelter, health care, and education. Oxfam provides relief in emergencies, and gives long-term support to people struggling to build a better life for themselves and their families.

Oxfam UK and Ireland works in Senegal funding, advising and collaborating with unions of village associations, groups of poor urban women, and the Senegalese union of non-governmental organizations. The programme aims to increase the ability of these groups to respond to the needs of those they represent. Oxfam funds, trains and helps groups influence local government policies. Activities supported include: small business projects, tree nurseries and tree planting, water supply, animal husbandry, grain banks, irrigation, literacy, milling and threshing.

The author and publishers would like to thank the following for their help in preparing this book: David Waller of Oxfam's West Africa Desk; Bob Gibson and François Diop and staff of Oxfam's Senegal office; Jenny Lunnon who gathered the information about Namarel and James Hawkins for the photographs; Ousemane Pam, Dikel Gadjiga, Fatou Oumar Seck, Mustapha Dia, Moussa Sow, Abdoulaye Gallo Bâ, Alassane Diouf, Dikkal Sow and all the people of ADENA (l'Association pour le Développement de Namarel); Aminata Abdoulaye Seck of Project Integré de Podor; Tracey Hawkins of Oxfam's photo library; and Ange Grunsell, Oxfam Primary Education Advisor, who commented on drafts.

The Oxfam Education Catalogue lists a range of other resources on economically developing countries, including Senegal, and issues of development. These materials are produced by Oxfam, by other agencies, and by Development Education Centres. For a copy of the catalogue contact Oxfam, 274 Banbury Road, Oxford OX2 7DZ, phone (01865) 311311, or your national Oxfam office.

Photographic acknowledgements

The author and publishers wish to acknowledge, with thanks, the following photographic sources:
D Brown/Oxfam p12; Alison Brownlie pp4, 6, 25; Jeremy Hartley/Oxfam pp5, 7, 8, 12c, 15, 24, 26, 28t, 29; James Hawkins pp10, 11, 15b, 16–23, 28b

The publishers have made every effort to trace the copyright holders, but if they have inadvertently overlooked any, they will be pleased to make the necessary arrangement at the first opportunity.

Cover photograph: Oxfam/James Hawkins

Note to the reader - In this book there are some words in the text which are printed in **bold** type. This shows that the word is listed in the glossary on page 30. The glossary gives a brief explanation of words which may be new to you.

First published in Great Britain by Heinemann Library, an imprint of Heinemann Publishers (Oxford) Ltd Halley Court, Jordan Hill, Oxford OX2 8EJ

OXFORD LONDON EDINBURGH MADRID ATHENS BOLOGNA PARIS MELBOURNE SYDNEY AUCKLAND SINGAPORE TOKYO IBADAN NAIROBI HARARE GABORONE PORTSMOUTH NH (USA)

© 1996 Heinemann Publishers (Oxford) Ltd

00 99 98 97 96
10 9 8 7 6 5 4 3 2 1

British Library Cataloguing in Publication Data
Brownlie, Alison
    Senegal. – (Worldfocus Series)
    I. Title II. Series
    966.3

ISBN 0 431 07248 5 (Hardback)

ISBN 0 431 07240 X (Paperback)

Designed and produced by Visual Image
Cover design by Threefold Design
Printed and bound in Britain by Bath Press Colourbooks, Glasgow

A 5% royalty on all copies of this book sold by Heinemann Publishers (Oxford) Ltd will be donated to Oxfam (United Kingdom and Ireland), a registered charity number 202918.